Police coloring book for Kids

THIS BOOK BELONGS TO:

HAVE FUN

POLICE

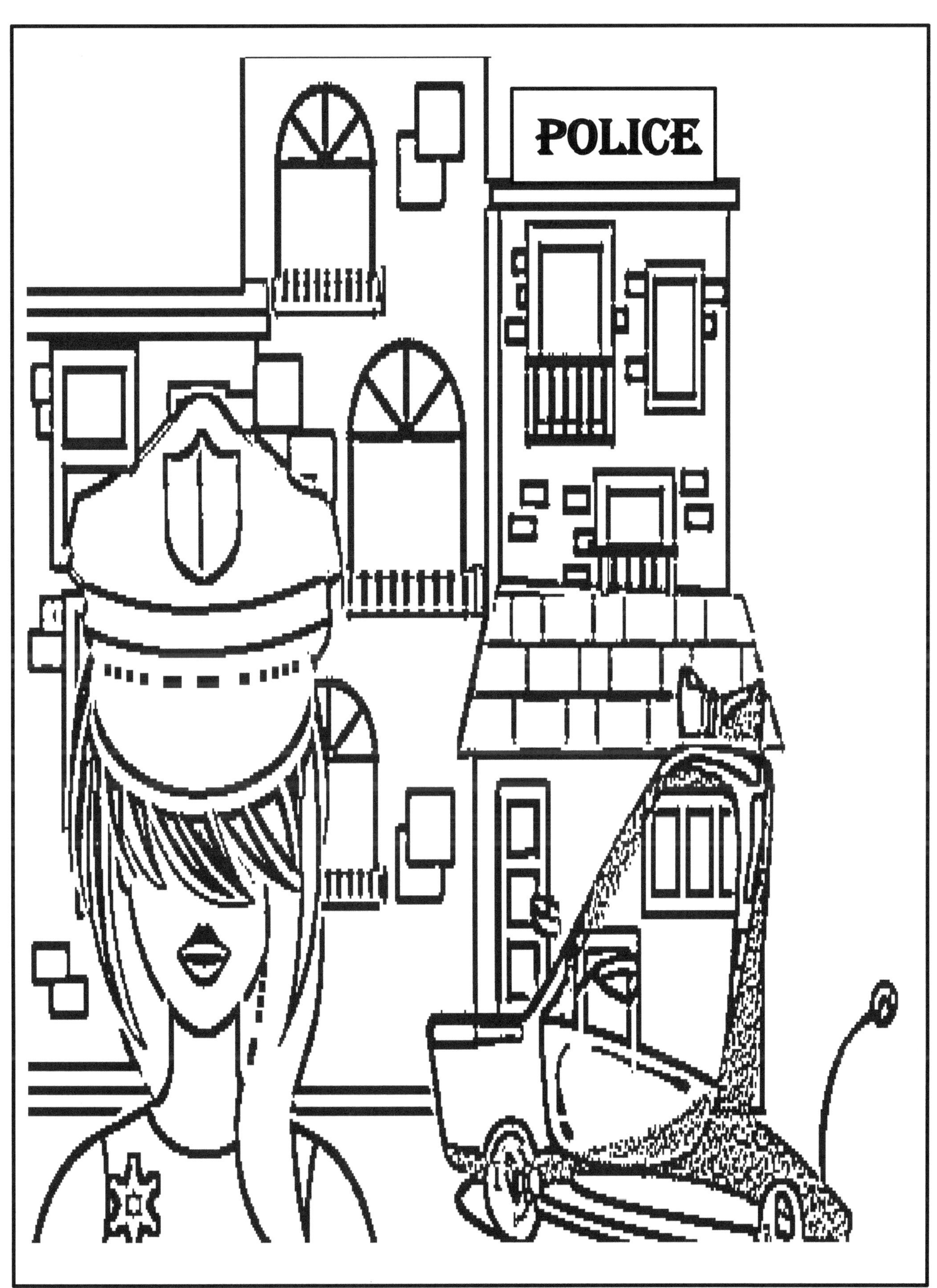

POLICE

POLICE

POLICE

POLICE

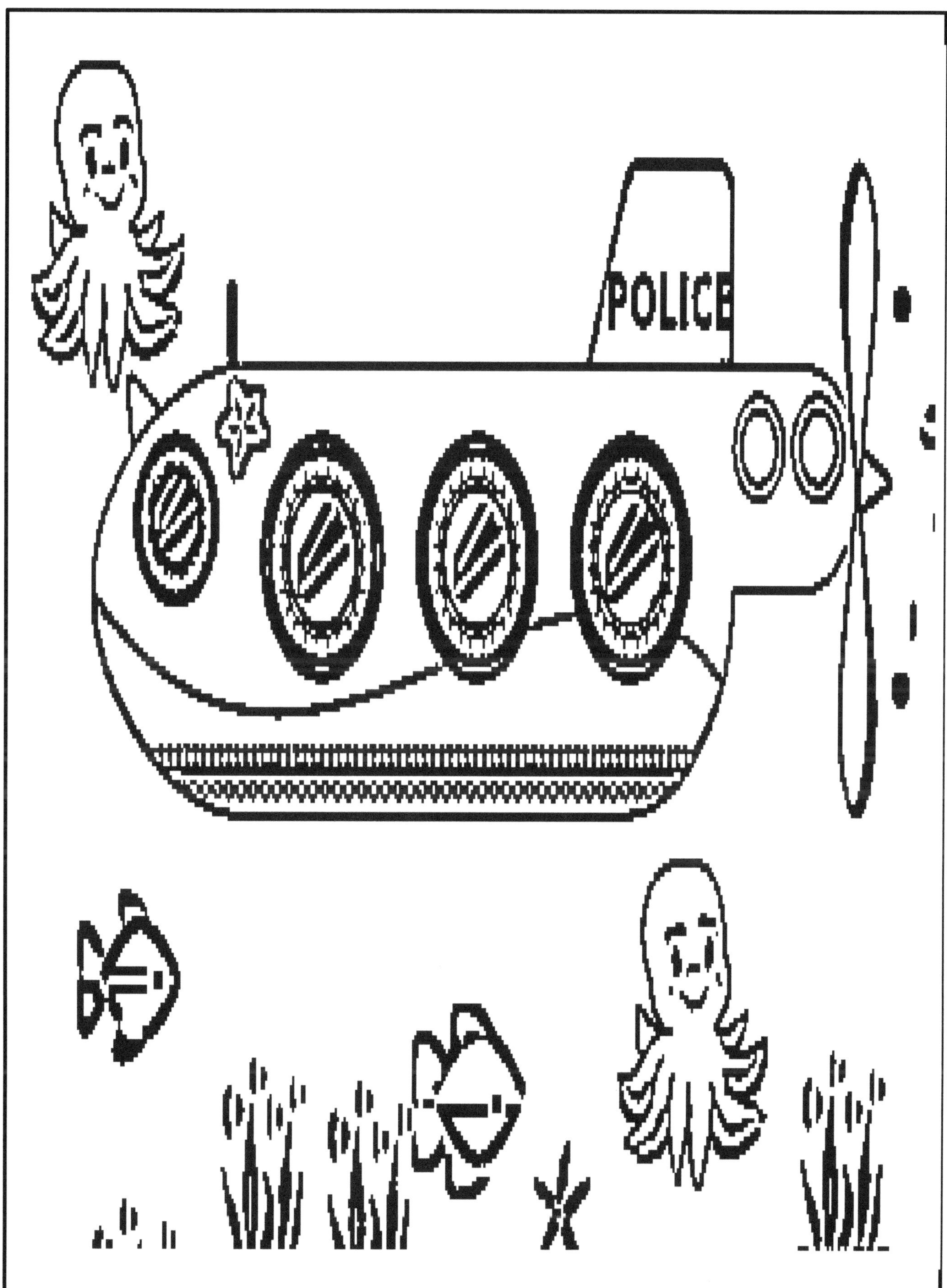
POLICE

POLICE

POLICE

police

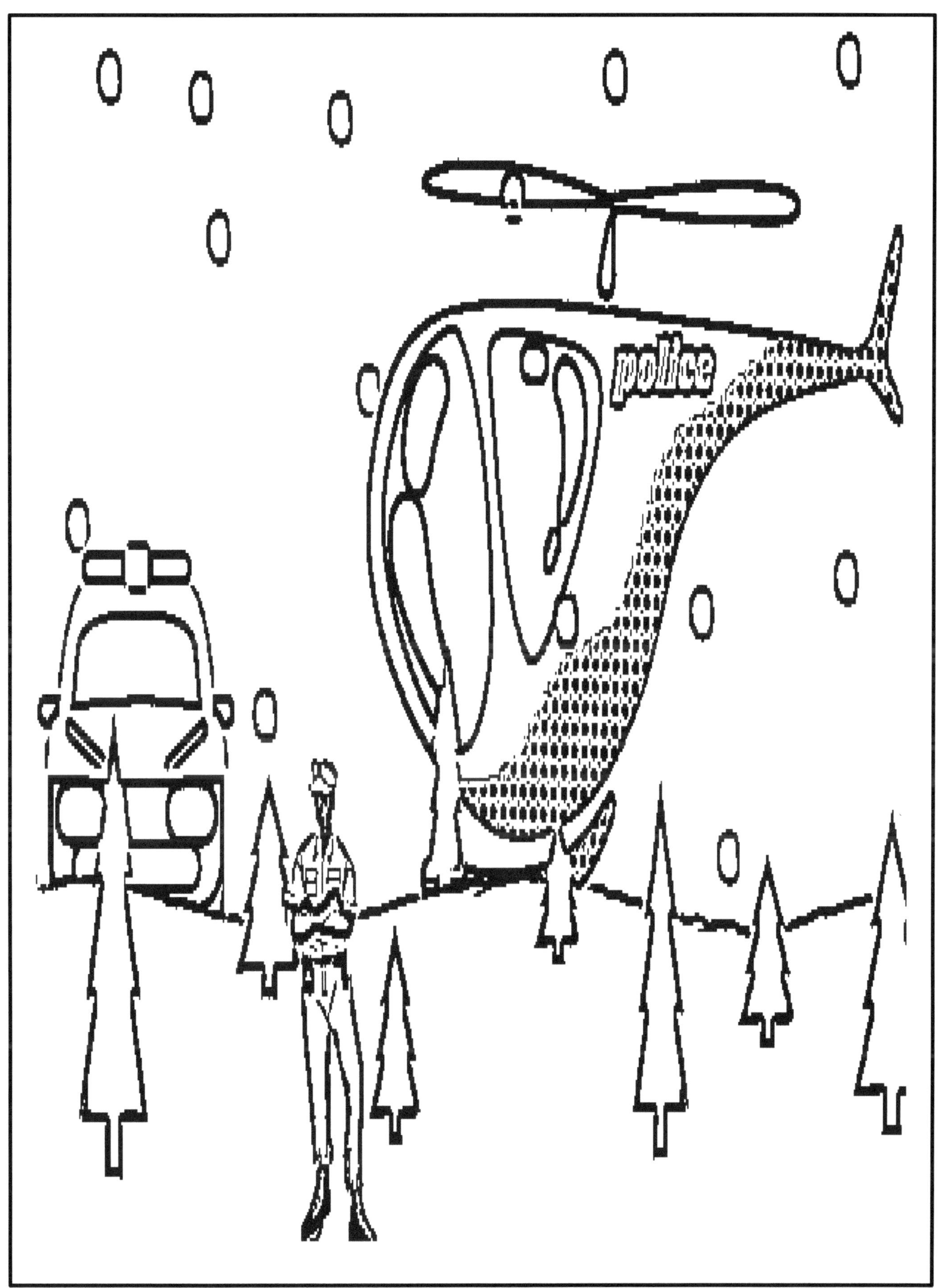

police

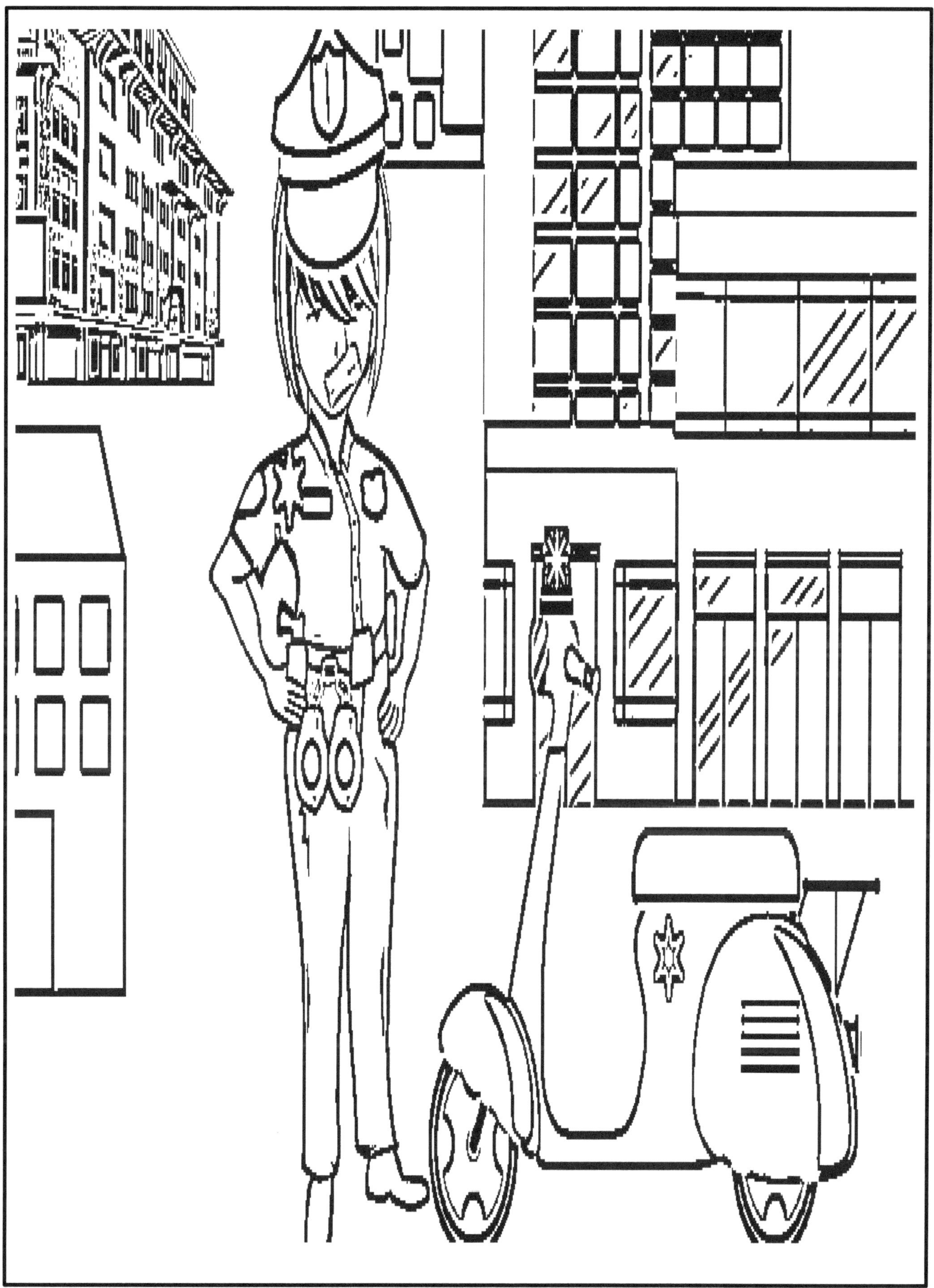

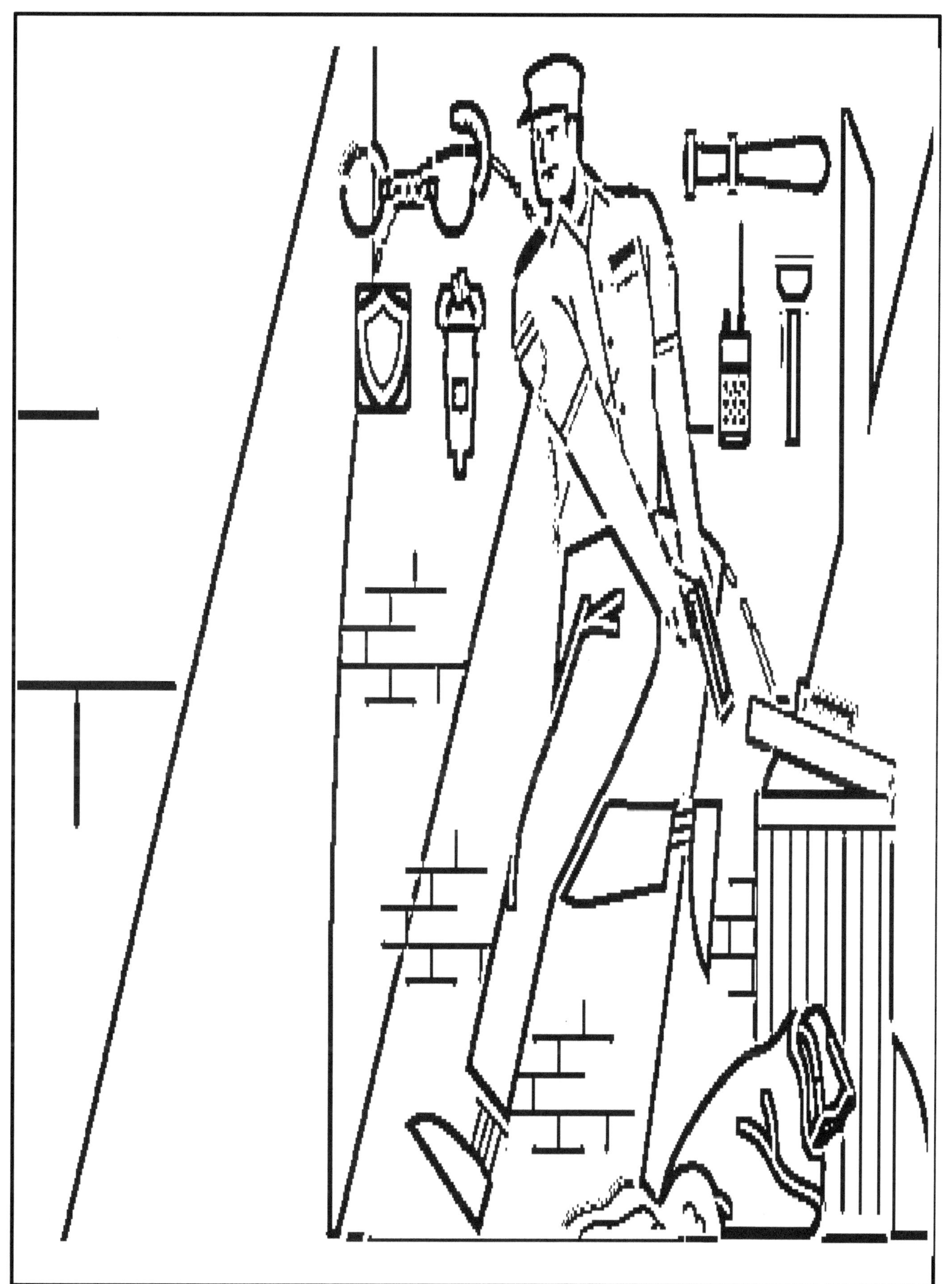

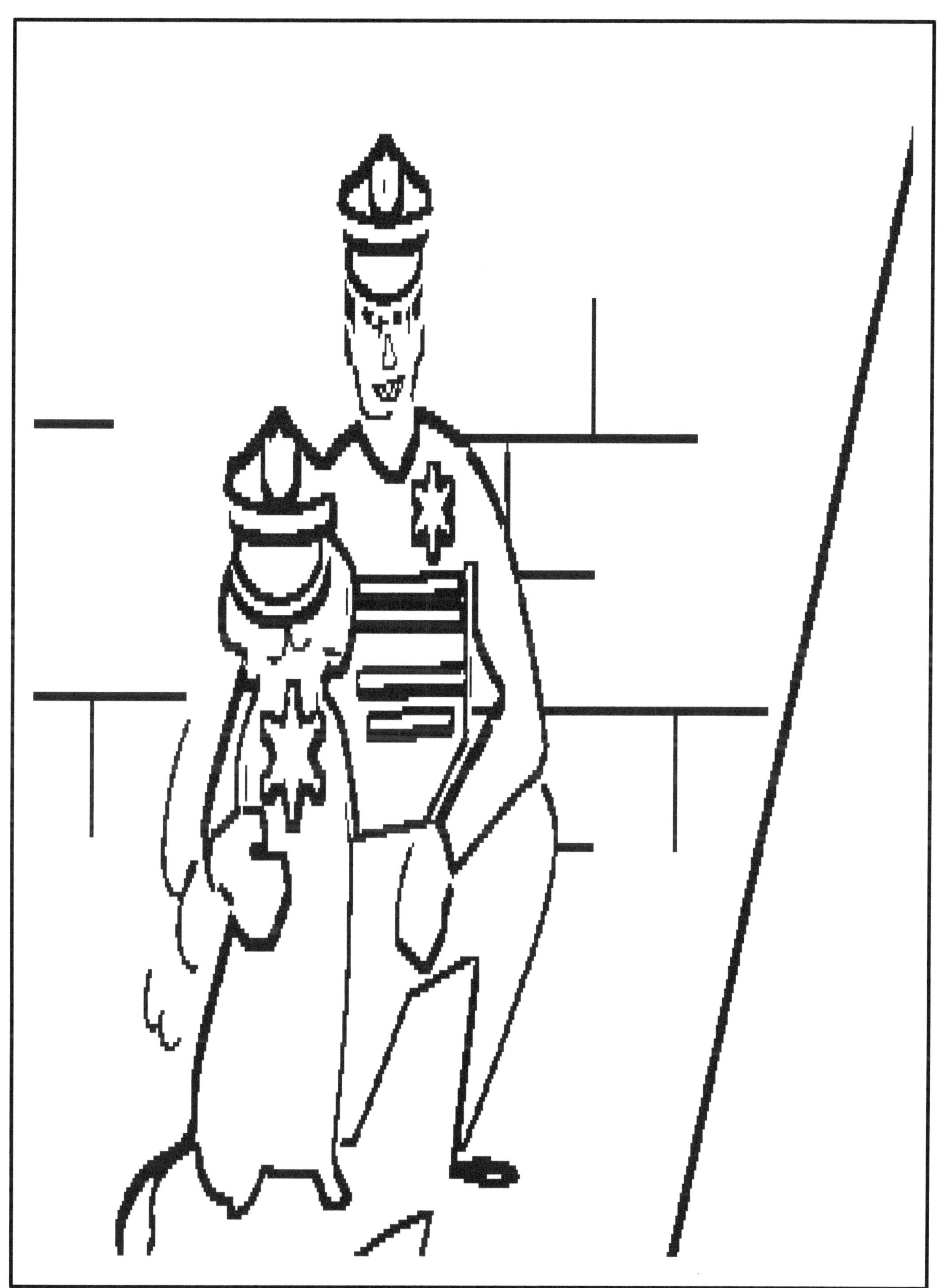

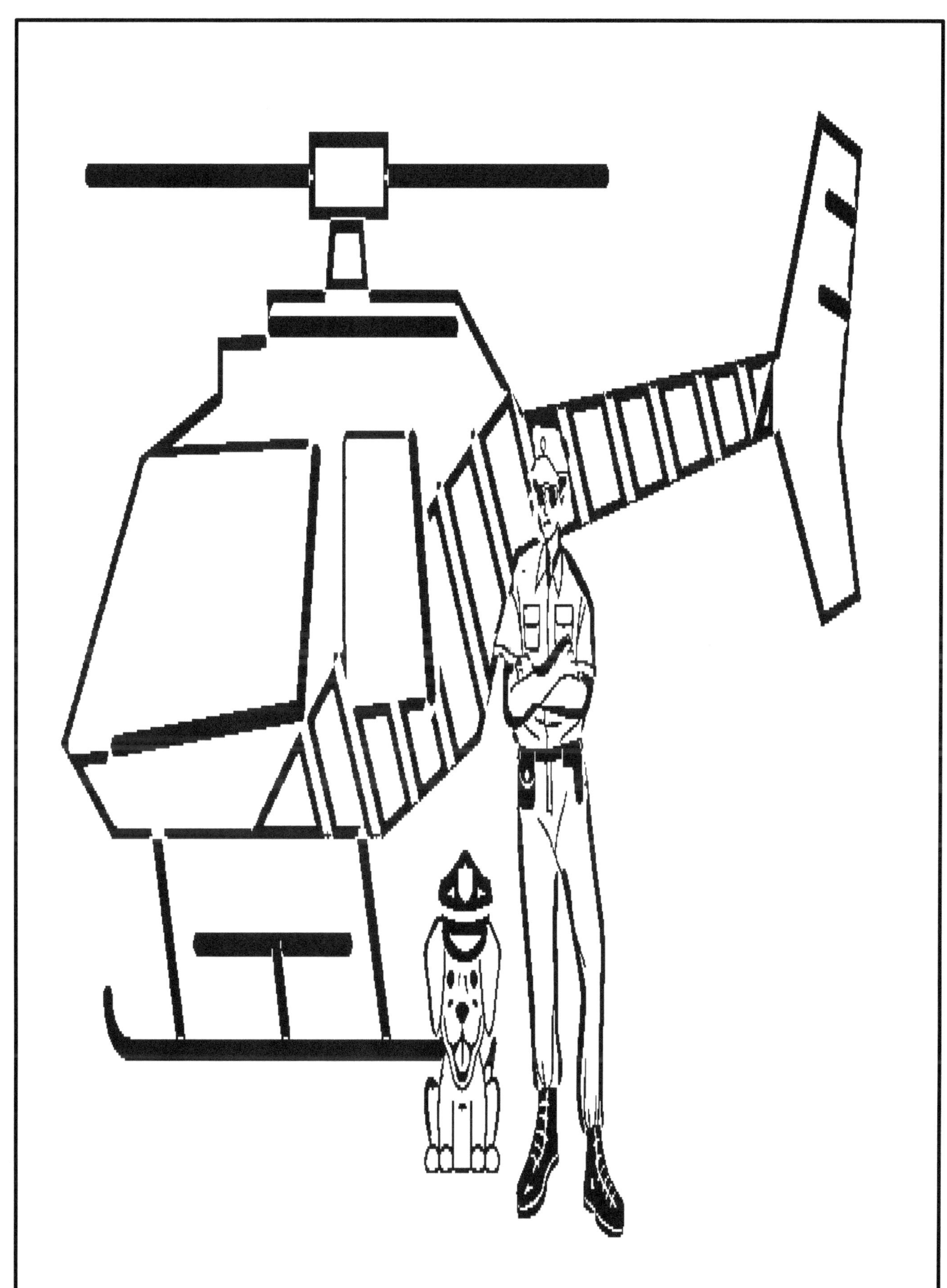

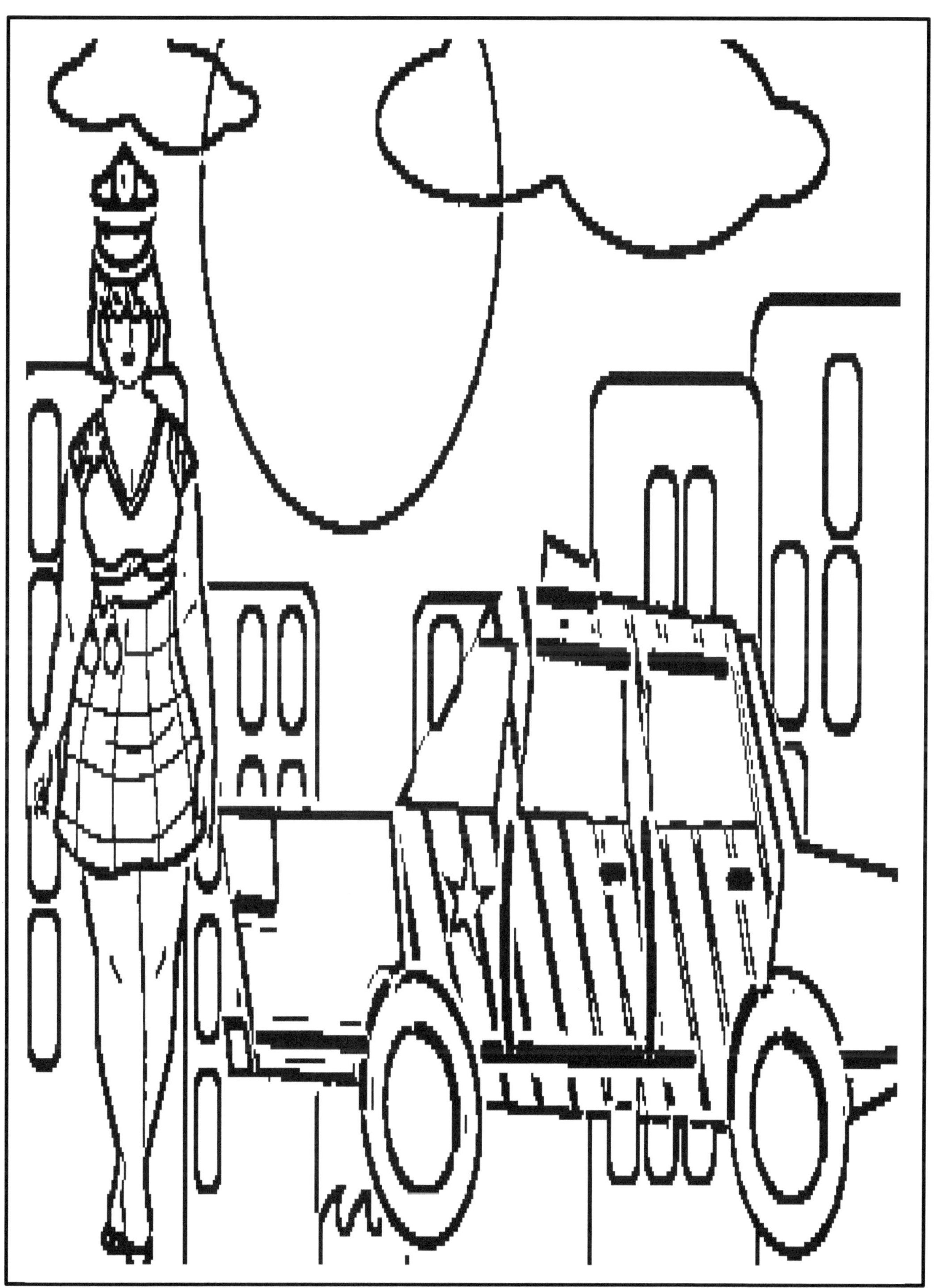

POLICE
POLICE

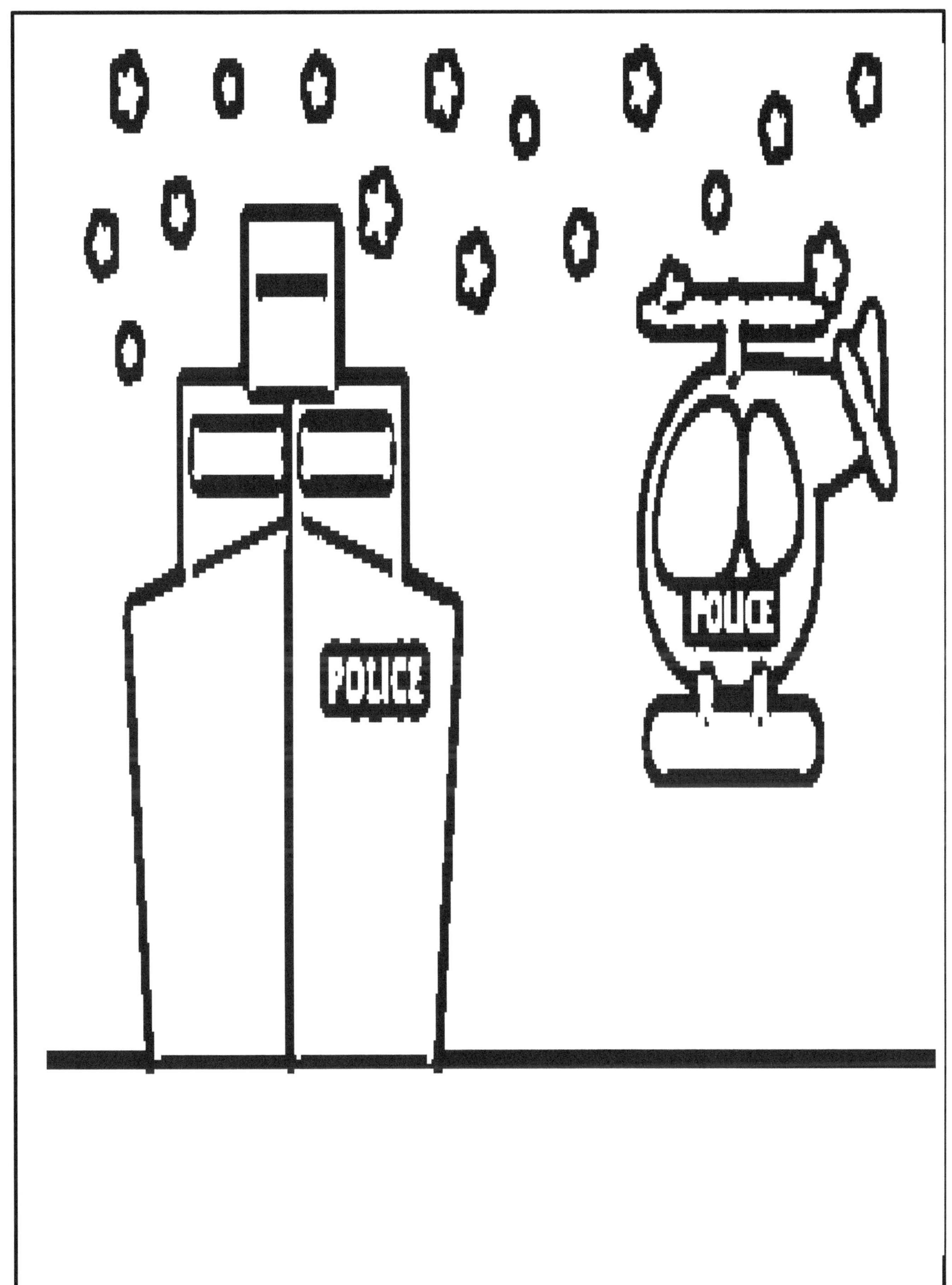
POLICE
POLICE

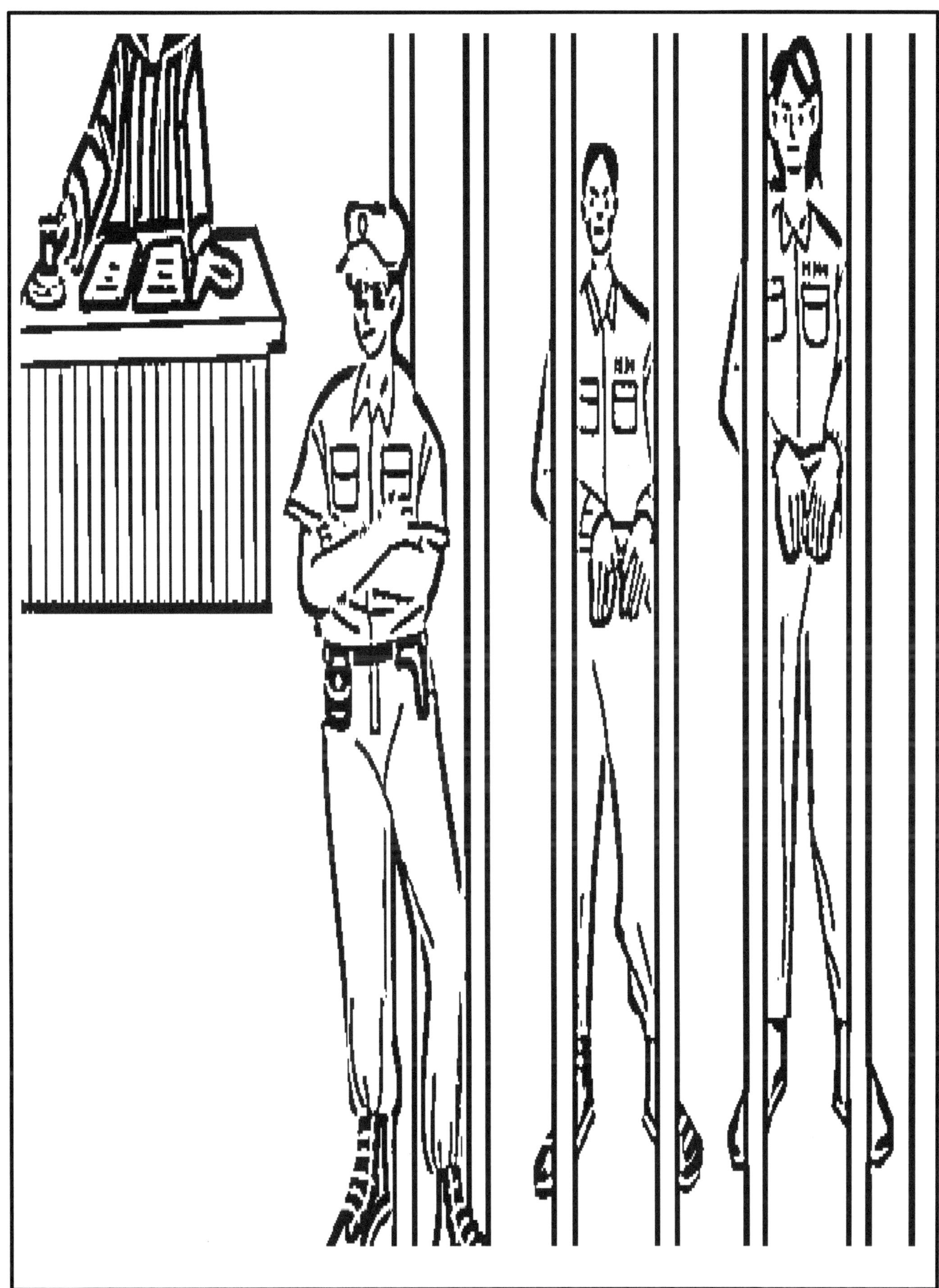

POLICE

POLICE

POLICE

POLICE